P9-DEY-539

Christmas with Rosamunde Pilcher

Christmas with Rosamunde Pilcher

Edited by
Siv Bublitz

Photos by
Andreas von Einsiedel

St. Martin's Press ❧ New York

A THOMAS DUNNE BOOK.
An imprint of St. Martin's Press.

Pictures: Bildschön Fotorecherche
Layout: Edith Lackmann
Styling: Dawn Williams
Collaborator/Consultant: Sara Lithgow
Jacket Design: Barbara Hanke (Photo by Andreas von Einsiedel)

Text translated by Erika Schmid from the German, except for "A Very Special Holiday"
and "Miss Cameron at Christmas"

ISBN 0-312-19247-9

Christmas with Rosamunde Pilcher was first published in Germany by Siv
Bublitz, an imprint of Rowohlt Verlag GmbH, under the title Weihnachten
mit Rosamunde Pilcher.

First U.S. Edition: October 1998

10 9 8 7 6 5 4 3 2 1

ontents

A Very Special Holiday   *1*

Christmas Cards   *21*

Christmas Baking   *31*

Final Preparations   *41*

Christmas Day   *49*

The Holiday Feast   *64*

"Miss Cameron at Christmas"   *85*

Acknowledgements   *121*

A Very Special Holiday

SUNDAY, 22ND DECEMBER, 1996

The tiny village of Zennor on the north cliffs of Cornwell. Only ten minutes from Lands End. Six o'clock in the evening and it is already dark. A frosty night, with a bitter wind blowing in from the Atlantic. We approach over the moor, find parking spaces in a lane narrow as a tunnel, unload, and then start walking, a straggling group of twelve persons, up the slope towards the church. The square tower of this glows with light from the floodlights which the publican, David Care, has set up in the car-park of the Tinners Arms.

Overhead, the bells ring out into the darkness, their sound tossed away by the wind. My youngest son is one of the bell-ringers. From various directions can be seen groups of muffled figures; torches and lanterns wink in the gloom; families, small children, young mothers carrying their

1

babies. We all converge to climb the flight of granite steps that lead into the graveyard, where stands the traditional tree, buffeted and shaken by gusts of salty air.

"Hello there! Some cold, isn't it?"

We pass through the door and down into the church, as though stepping into a cave. Tiny, granite, chilled with age, lit by candles, and the air sharp with the scent of fir and green holly. Gradually the pews are filling up, with farmers, teachers, painters, potters, old folk and young families, many of them in some way or another related to my husband. Their children wear woollen hats and scarves and gloves, and eyes shine with wonder and anticipation.

It is a service of lessons and carols. Because this evening we have no priest, each lesson is read by a member of the community, standing there in working clothes, jeans and casual jackets, checked shirts, trainers. But the carols we all sing, led by an organist who doubles his duties with that of chorus-master.

"Oh come, all ye Faithful . . ."

A gust of wind thumps at the church with a howl and then a great clout.

". . . Joyful and triumphant . . ."

St. Uny Church in Lelant, where Rosamunde and Graham Pilcher were married.

The beginning of Christmas.

As a child, I was never a great fan of Christmas. For various very good reasons it was always rather a low-key and disappointing time, and my memories of it are encapsulated by the smell of the little village post office, warmed by paraffin heaters and set about with open boxes of Christmas cards, which cost a halfpenny, a penny, or twopence, according to how generous you happened to be feeling. As well, Christmas came in midwinter, and winter was not my favourite time. The house dark and full of shadows, the wind rattling the window panes, and, out of doors, naked tree branches tossing their heads against the cheerless skies.

My husband and I were married on December 7, 1946, in the church of St. Uny, Lelant, in Cornwall. I was born in Lelant and had been christened in that church, but Graham came from Scotland. He had, however,

strong family connections with St. Ives and Zennor, and so the church was filled more with his many relations than with mine.

Fifty years later, and Golden Wedding time. How to celebrate? Lately, we had thrown two large parties. A seventieth-birthday party (mine) and an eightieth- (Graham's). Yet another elaborate luncheon for our loved but elderly friends did not seem the most brilliant of ideas. So instead it was decided that we should take the children, and their children, for a week to a hotel in St. Ives, for the week of Christmas.

The count came to fourteen. From London, Fiona and Will and his two sons. From Scotland, ourselves, Robin and Kirsty, and their four children. Mark and Jess live in Zennor and so were already there. Only Pippa was missing. She and her husband and five children were in Maui, Hawaii, and it was tacitly agreed that half-way around the world was a little too far to travel, even for such an important occasion.

On the shortest day of the year, the Scottish contingent travelled by train from Dundee to Penzance. Most of the journey was in darkness and the sun only slid up into the sky for long enough for us to admire a gloomy view of the Midlands, not the most exciting bit of Britain. At the junction we were met by Mark and Jess's father, who filled their cars with us and our considerable luggage and drove us to St. Ives. There is a special moment on this short journey, when the road slips downhill between trees and the view opens up—the great bay, the distant lighthouse, and, far below, the curve of the harbour, twinkling with reflected lights. The way it had always looked on cold midwinter evenings, and I rolled down the window and smelt the salt of the sea on the cold air. A half moon was

rising from behind Godrevy, and the black ocean was feathered with silver light.

The hotel we had chosen was comfortingly familiar. I had come here often as a child, for Christmas parties, and sometimes, during the war, spent leaves there with my parents, because our own house had been let for the duration to a family evacuated from London. Because of this I always thought gratefully of the sanctuary it had once offered, as well as festivities . . . associations of party frocks, dancing pumps, jellies and crackers. Playing Pass-the-Parcel, and dancing Sir Roger de Coverley. Sixty years later, it felt much the same: bright with Christmas decorations, music playing from somewhere, and a feeling in the air of innocent excitement and anticipation. Our arrival added to all this, as well as increasing, by several decibels, the noise level. Bedrooms were sorted out and inspected, cousins reunited, television sets turned on full blast, and hot baths run.

The manager appeared, not to complain, but to welcome us. I said, "I hope we don't make too much noise!" but clearly nobody minded, and that was the way it was for the whole seven days.

The weather, magically, was beautiful. Very cold and windy, but clear-skied, so that St. Ives was washed in pale luminous sunshine. I had forgot-

ten the little town in midwinter, had not been here at Christmas time since the year before the war, and was astonished to discover how little it had actually changed. Scoured by the winds, bleached of tourists, and with many shops and cafés firmly closed, the narrow streets and the harbour came into their own again, and it was possible to observe the shape and proportions of the old houses, the streets and quays, and to make one's way with ease down the baffling cobbled lanes, where the wind funnelled as though down a chimney and the floating gulls screamed overhead. The children disappeared on secret missions, to buy last-minute Christmas presents, packets of sweets and dark-red nail varnish, and the bigger boys made their way to Porthmeor Beach where the surfers, like seals in their black wet-suits, rode the breakers on Porthmeor Beach.

In all this activity the Golden Wedding lost some of its significance. But, of course, there had to be a party, organized by Fiona, Robin, and Mark, who had spent secret months putting it all together. It took place on Monday evening, the day before Christmas Eve, and the venue was the Carbis Bay Hotel, closed for the season, but opened especially for us, which meant that we had the dining room to ourselves. The Carbis Bay Hotel stands on the beach, a stately Victorian edifice built at the time of the newly arrived railway line, its approach a steep winding hill running

down from the main road. As the taxis (prudently ordered) trundled us down this hill, the moon, now full as a plate, rose in the cloudless sky and washed everything in silver. Entering, we found the hotel en fête: champagne corks popping, a jazz band playing music from our time, long tables set, flowers and Christmas lights, and the gleam of silver and glass. Sixty friends and relations were gathered to help us celebrate . . . many had been at our wedding, but most of them had been born since that day. One bridesmaid managed to make it, but our best man, for some reason, had been lost in the mists of time, and nobody knew if he was even still alive.

It was a good party. For days after, it was talked about as one of the best. A delicious meal, flowing and carefully chosen wine, a celebration cake (excellent). Speeches (not very good). The jazz band played and everybody danced. Then the band departed for some refreshment, and my son Robin took over. He borrowed a guitar, sang a few songs, delivered a poem for us which he had written that afternoon, and finally gathered his wife and sister to sing with him the old Everly Brothers song, "Dream, Dream, Dream," a party turn they had all been doing since they were teenagers.

The next morning everybody was a bit quiet at breakfast, and there were a few sore heads. However, it was another day of spring-like beauty, and it was decided that fresh air and exercise were the order of the day.

At Carbis Bay we had left the remains of the celebration cake as well as the silver salver on which it sat, so we gathered together a party of walkers. This did not include the boys, who had ordered breakfast in bed, were having a long lie-in, watching TV and didn't even want to hear the words "fresh air."

To get to Carbis Bay, we walked along the cliffs. The sea below us was blue as summer, lapping at the edge of the cliffs, and we went past gardens bathed in sunlight, filled with camellias and palm trees, and tall clumps of Monterey pines which soughed in the breeze overhead. The children ran on ahead and down onto the beach, and there was a man walking his dog, their footsteps stitching a line on sand washed and ironed by the ebb tide.

On Christmas morning our room was invaded by grandchildren, each bearing a bulging stocking.

In no time, the room was awash with wrappings, ribbons, empty teacups, trinkets, teddy bears, false noses and tangerine peel. The smell of tangerines is one of the true smells of Christmas. After an enormous breakfast, out to Zennor again for morning service, which ended, traditionally, by the entire congregation streaming across the road and into the Tinners Arms. Because this is so small, and there are so many people, it swiftly becomes extremely warm, noisy and convivial, and we would probably have spent the entire afternoon there, except that we had to be back in St. Ives in time for Christmas lunch. Rounding up a party of so many people takes a bit of organizing and it was not until we reached the hotel that we could be certain no small child had inadvertently been left behind.

The remains of the day are spent eating food, opening presents, taking a long constitutional walk on the beach, watching television, playing pool, getting dressed up, eating yet another enormous meal, and finally dancing the night away with our fellow guests. There is a disco. After a lot of funky rock, the disc jockey plays a barn dance, and then an eightsome reel, after which he persuades my son-in-law to do an imitation of Tom Jones, into which he throws his all. It is not until the small hours that everybody, including the yawning youngest, finally falls into bed.

The remainder of the week slips by in the manner of all holidays. Days merge into days, so that dissociated vignettes, beyond chronology, stay in the mind.

"The sea, as blue as in summer, lapped at the steep cliffs."

Going to Mark's farm, to view progress. Gear, when he bought it eighteen months ago, consisted of a small farmhouse with an adjacent barn and broken-down outbuildings. By Christmas 1996, the great renovation was just about halfway through: the house and barn joined, the slates on the roof; inside, the shell of the new interior; outside, mud, rubble, destruction worthy of Bosnia at its worst. But yet, in the heart of the old house, the original kitchen still stands. Logs blaze in the great granite fireplace, the beamed ceiling is low, their Christmas tree twinkles with light. Tea and fruit-cake on the kitchen table, all of us sitting around and speculating on how long the work will take; how to furnish the beautiful new sitting-room, where to build a sheltered garden.

Time spent with my eldest grandson, whose ambition is to be accepted for a four-year course at the Edinburgh School of Art. We walk together down into St. Ives and through the baffling maze of Downalong, calling in at every art gallery with a door standing open. We end up at the new Tate, a temple of a building, erected on Porthmeor Beach on the site of the old town gasworks. The interior is so beautiful that the paintings are somehow of second importance, but always there are new and fascinating exhibitions. When we tire of looking, we go up to the restaurant and drink coffee, not talking much but watching the rollers break on the white sands of the beach below us.

"I should like," he says at last, "to come back and paint."

I say, "You probably will," and in the gallery shop, I buy him a book on Barbara Hepworth.

On our only grey day, lunch at Tremedda. Tremedda, once the home of Graham's Aunt Elsie, and where he spent many of his boyhood summers. A walk on the cliffs across the misty, baffling fields, patchworked by Bronze Age walls and already touched with yellow—the first flowers of the gorse. Then lunch in the farmhouse kitchen—so many of us that there aren't enough chairs, nor space at the table. After, a football match, fathers versus sons, and unlikely relations called in as umpires and goalkeepers.

Finally, our last day and back to Lelant. The sun has come out again. The sheltered village, where violets used to be grown, scenting all the air with their nostalgic perfume, feels spring-like with unseasonable warmth. We lunch at The Badger, and afterwards set out walking down the hill to the little railway station and The Elms, where I spent the first twelve years of my life. Then along the lane to the church, and so across the golf links to the sea. The dunes are empty, the beach deserted, the tide far out. We can just hear the waves curling in over the distant margins of the shore. The children climb the dunes and leap down the long gullies of sand, and the high-tide line is a treasure trove of shells. On the way back to the cars, we go into the church and write in the battered Visitors Book. "50 years ago we were married here." We sign our names.

It seems, all at once, a very long time.

We return to Scotland, as we had come. By train. Black early morning and we wait on the platform at the junction, until the great intercity engine comes streaming through the cutting from Penzance. Aboard, we settle sleepily down, none of us inclined to talk. The rain flings itself at the glass of the windows, and beyond, all is darkness.

And I know that coming back was a good idea. A success. It had worked. No spats. No family squabbles. Only laughter. And as Hayle and Camborne slid away behind us and the sky gradually began to lighten, I recalled those bleak Christmases of childhood and knew now that they were no longer of any importance. Had been cancelled out, obliterated by perhaps the best Christmas ever.

Rosamunde Pilcher

Christmas Cards

For Rosamunde Pilcher, the Christmas season begins in November, when she writes her first Christmas cards. Roughly three hundred friends, relatives, and acquaintances all over the world receive Christmas greetings from her, and to make sure no one is forgotten, she has a long list of names and addresses to remind her. At the beginning of November, when darkness descends on Scotland, already early in the afternoon, she sits down at her desk and takes out the list.

Letters to go overseas come first. Rosamunde Pilcher's daughter Pippa lives with her husband and five children in the United States. To be sure greetings and presents will be under the tree on Christmas Day, they will have to be mailed by mid-November the latest. The same holds true for the many friends and relatives of the Pilcher family in Australia, New Zealand, Canada, and India. "I enjoy writing Christmas cards," says Rosamunde. "Even though you haven't seen someone for a long time, it's nice to get in touch once a year and keep the relationship alive. Whenever I write to someone, my innermost thoughts are with that person. Memories are stirred up; it's like sharing an intimate moment with someone you perhaps might rarely see again. I relish this feeling, and it puts me in a festive mood right away."

The custom of sending holiday greetings with good wishes dates back to antiquity. In ancient Rome people would exchange small gifts at New Year's: olive branches, dried fruit, honey, coins and other good-luck charms. Later, Christians would move this practice to the Christmas season. And not long after the invention of the printing press, the Christmas card made its appearance. At first the hand-decorated cards bore reli-

As early as November Rosamunde Pilcher mails the first cards and presents overseas.

Christmas cards have been known in England since the nineteenth century. Besides the "classic" robin and Father Christmas, there are many much-beloved motifs. Today, old Christmas cards have become sought-after collector's items.

Happiness be thine this CHRISTMAS DAY.

Christmas Joys.

A VERY MERRY CHRISTMAS.

Simple diet is best, for many dishes bring many diseases and rich sauces are worse than even heaping several meals upon each other.

Xmas Wishes

WE HAIL THE JOYOUS DAY ONCE M

ght and
py
mas

❄ A MERRY CHRISTMAS ❄

CHEERY GREETINGS

Allow me, Miss!

Wishing you a happy Christmas

Loving
CHRISTMAS
Greetings.

May your
Christmas
be Jolly.

Rosamunde Pilcher decorates
the whole house with the
Christmas cards she receives.
Shown here is an alcove in
the dining room.

gious motifs, but gradually flowers, birds, and ornaments were added. In England, the first commercially produced Christmas card appeared in 1843, as Great Britain adopted the Continental tradition of celebrating Christmas as a family holiday. After Queen Victoria married the German Prince Albert of Saxe-Coburg-Gotha in 1840, the English court began to observe Christmas in the traditional German way, with a decorated tree and a festive dinner on Christmas Day. Family life was highly rated in Victorian England, and the idea of a family-centreed holiday was enthusiastically embraced. The first mass-produced Christmas card shows a typically Victorian family scene with parents, children, and grandparents, all peaceably gathered around a richly laden dinner-table. Then and now, however, the favourite subject of British Christmas cards has been the robin, closely followed by Father Christmas, the English Santa Claus. In addition to these two "classic" motifs, there were quite a few others, which, over the years, have undergone rather strange style changes. For instance, at the turn of the century people displayed a morbid attraction for dead birds lying in snow, a sight that moved Victorian ladies to tears and seemed to stir Christmassy nostalgia in them.

At first, Christmas cards were sent only to faraway friends and relatives, but nowadays we mail Christmas and New Year greetings even to our neighbours. Every year, Rosamunde receives several

English Christmas card in fan shape, ca. 1920.

hundred Christmas cards, which she displays all over the house. "I enjoy every single one," she says, "and it would be a shame just to let the cards lie around somewhere unappreciated. Of course, only a few will fit on the mantelpiece, but I also decorate the alcoves in the drawing room and the dining room with cards; or I attach several of them on pretty silk ribbons that I hang from the walls."

The Christmas season begins with the writing of the first holiday greeting, and the cards that are received become the first Christmas decorations in the house.

"It is almost as if we surround ourselves with the people who are close to us," says Rosamunde. "And isn't that a wonderful way to ring in the Christmas season?"

Rosamunde Pilcher enjoys looking at her Christmas cards again and again. "It's a little as if your loved ones were gathered around you."

Christmas Baking

Rosamunde Pilcher doesn't really care much for sweets, and baking is not exactly her cup of tea. But she makes an exception during the Christmas season. "I love the scent of scones and mince pies as it wafts through the house. Besides, the smell usually draws the whole family to the kitchen, and we share this warm and cozy feeling."

The kitchen, in the spacious house near Dundee in Scotland, has plenty of room both for cooking and eating. It is comfortably warm even on the coldest days, thanks to the Aga, the typically British gas-fired stove, which is actually more an oven whose fire is never allowed to die down in the winter. There are several chambers for baking and to keep foods warm, and the constantly kept hot stove surface is covered by several heavy enamel plates, which only have to be removed as needed. Thus a kettle of water for tea will heat up in no time at all. At a pinch, the Aga will even do duty as a clothes airer, with the folded garment laid on the shining hob-cover, or hung over the upper rail.

When baking, Rosamunde usually follows old family recipes that have been handed down from generation to generation. Among her favourites are Scottish specialties like drop scones or oatcakes. She stores the biscuits in large tins, which she keeps on the "dresser," the large old sideboard in her kitchen. "They are there for anyone to help him-

Rosamunde Pilcher in the kitchen of her house near Dundee. In the background at left the Aga.

self, and usually the tins are emptied fairly quickly," says the author. Whenever guests are invited for tea, the supply must be replenished. Sometimes she finds this a bit laborious—as we know, baking is not her most favourite pastime. But then everyone gathers in the kitchen again, there's the sweet smell of scones, the Aga exudes its cosy warmth . . . "When I gladly begin to bake and actually enjoy it," says Rosamunde, "then I know it will soon be Christmas."

A tip from *Rosamunde Pilcher*:

A small glass, such as a sherry glass, is ideal to cut out the scones.

Scones

4 cups/500 g. flour

1 teaspoon baking powder

pinch of salt

4 tablespoons/60 g. soft butter

1⅓ cups/300 ml. buttermilk

Sift together flour, baking powder, and salt. Knead in butter, then add buttermilk gradually, using a fork or the back of a knife to mix the dough until it is soft but not sticky. Roll out on a floured board to a thickness of about an inch, or slightly more. Cut out circles and bake in a 400-degree F. oven on the top rack for about fifteen minutes, till the scones have risen and are golden-brown. Cut scones in half and serve with whipped cream, crème fraiche, or butter and strawberry jam.

Granddaughter Alice helps
with the Christmas baking.

Drop Scones

¾ cup/100 g. flour

½ teaspoon baking powder

5 oz./150 ml. milk

pinch of salt

1 egg

3 tablespoons sugar

Sift together flour, baking powder, salt and sugar. Press down center of dry ingredients to form hollow to receive egg. Quickly mix with a wooden spoon, adding milk gradually, to create a thick-flowing crêpe batter. Butter a large skillet and heat up gently over a low flame. With a tablespoon drop batter into pan, being careful scones do not run together; one tablespoon equals one scone. (Rosamunde Pilcher bakes up to five drop scones at a time in her skillet—beginners should try two at first.) As soon as bubbles appear on the surface, turn scones and bake another two minutes, until both sides are nicely browned. Then lift them out and set them on a baking rack, within the folds of a clean dish towel. Drop scones must be eaten warm, served with butter and jam or honey.

Drop scones—these little pancakes are baked on the stove and eaten warm with butter.

Oatcakes

2 cups/225 g. oatmeal

1 teaspoon baking powder

pinch of salt

2 teaspoons melted butter
   or lard

5 fl. oz./150 ml. hot water

Mix oatmeal, baking powder, and salt. Add melted butter and water and mix well. Dust hands with oatmeal and knead dough well. On a floured board, roll out as thinly as possible. Cut out circles and place carefully on a parchment-paper-lined baking tin. Bake about twenty minutes at 375 degrees F.

Shortbread

10 oz./250 g. butter, softened

¾ cup/140 g. sugar

2¾ cups/380 g. flour

pinch of salt

Beat together butter and sugar, and salt. Knead in flour. Cover dough and let rest in refrigerator for two hours. Roll out chilled dough about 1 inch thick and lay onto a parchment-paper-lined baking tin. Shape a rim out of foil to make sure dough will not run out of tin. Prick with fork and bake at 375 degrees F. for 30 minutes. While hot, cut into thin, 2-inch-long strips.

Tip from Rosamunde Pilcher:

An easier way to make shortbread is to shape the dough into a roll about an inch thick before letting it rest in refrigerator. Cut off ½-inch-wide circles and lay them on baking tin. This way the biscuits do not have the typical strip shape, but they taste just as good.

Whisky Loaf

½ cup/115 ml. Scotch whisky

ground rind of 1 lemon

ground rind of 1 orange

3½ oz./100 g. candied fruit, chopped

3½ oz./100 g. raisins

6 oz./170 g. butter

½ cup/80 g. brown sugar

2 eggs, separated

2 cups/280 g. flour

1 teaspoon baking powder

Syrup

2½ oz./60 g. brown sugar

3 oz./85 ml. water

1 teaspoon whisky

Soak lemon- and orange peel, candied fruit, and raisins in whisky overnight.

Cream butter and sugar. Add egg yolks. Sift flour and baking powder together and add to butter mixture.

Add chopped fruits. Beat egg whites until stiff and add. Put dough into a buttered 1½-quart loaf pan and bake in a 350-degree F. oven for 120–135 minutes.

For syrup, dissolve sugar in water over a low flame, simmer 3–5 minutes. Remove from fire, add whisky. Prick the still-warm cake with a needle and pour warm syrup over it. Let cool in pan before unmoulding.

Mince pies—delicious at a pre-Christmas tea.

Mince Pies

These sweet pastries are a must on every tea-table in England and Scotland during the Christmas season. In Great Britain the filling can be bought ready-made everywhere. The little tins for the pies measure a little over 2 inches across the bottom and about 4 inches across the top rim, which is almost an inch high. The tins can be bought in stores specializing in housewares.

Mincemeat

(makes about 3 lbs.)

¾ lbs./350 g. tart apples

9 oz./225 g. dark raisins

5 oz./125 g. currants

9 oz./225 g. golden raisins

4 oz./100 g. candied lemon peel

(about) 8 oz./225 g. brown sugar

1 oz./25 g. chopped almonds

8 oz./225 g. beef suet or lard

salt

juice and ground peel of 1 lemon

3 tablespoons brandy, whisky, or rum

pinch of ground cloves, nutmeg,
    cinnamon, and Cayenne pepper

Peel and core apples and cut into chunks. Mix with the other chopped fruits and stir in sugar, suet or lard, almonds, lemon juice and rind, and spices. Cover bowl with a tea-towel and let sit for two to three days, stirring the mixture occasionally. Add alcohol, fill into glass jars, and close them. (Will keep about 6 weeks.)

$\mathscr{P}$ie $\mathscr{D}$ough (Pâté Brisée Sucrée)
(for 1 lb. mincemeat; makes 18–20 pies)
1½ cups/200 g. flour
4 oz. (½ cup)/100 g. butter
2 oz. (¼ cup)/50 g. sugar
pinch of salt
1 egg
1 egg white
sugar to sprinkle on

Combine flour, sugar, and salt. With two knives, or in a food processor, cut butter into dry ingredients until mixture has the consistency of coarse meal. Add whole egg.

Roll out dough thinly. Cut out circles measuring about 3 inches across and insert into tart shells. Fill about halfway with mincemeat. Cut out somewhat smaller circles for the top crust. Moisten rims with cold water to seal edges and carefully lay tops over the pies. Cut a small hole into top crust, then brush with egg white and sprinkle with sugar. Bake about 20 minutes in a 425-degree F. oven. When cool, serve with whipped cream.

Final Preparations

Contrary to German custom, where Christmas starts on Christmas Eve, in Great Britain the festivities start December 25. The day before Christmas is for last-minute preparations and shopping, especially since most stores keep the same hours as on normal week-days. Of course Rosamunde avoids as much as possible having to shop the day before Christmas. "It's too hectic; besides, there isn't much of a selection left. I might pick up the pre-ordered turkey at the butcher's; everything else has usually been taken care of."

No one in the Pilcher family gets upset or stressed out on this last day before the festivities. Rosamunde does without some special trappings rather than have her serenity disturbed by nervous bustling. "I feel Christmas should be a warm, cosy holiday above all. Guests as well as hosts should feel comfortable and at ease and enjoy the time they spend together."

Rosamunde's son Robin also lives with his family near Dundee. The grandchildren Alice, Hugo, and Florence spend a lot of time with Grandmother, and Christmas is often celebrated at her house. The other three Pilcher children usually spend the holiday with their own families: Mark, the youngest Pilcher son, lives in Cornwall; daughter Fiona in London; and her sister Philippa, nicknamed Pippa, in Long Island or Maui, Hawaii.

On Christmas Eve the last presents are packed.

Before the children arrive to decorate the tree, Rosamunde likes to enjoy the quiet calm of the day before Christmas. She wraps a last few presents and takes a final look at the decorations with which she has adorned the whole house. Here she doesn't strive to achieve anything grand or elaborate. "I don't believe in revamping the whole house at Christmas and to put needle-shedding branches everywhere. A few small ornaments are easy to fashion and yet they can create a very festive atmosphere."

The author treasures beautiful Christmas decorations and uses them year after year, but something new is always added: colourful balls, gold-sprayed pinecones and twigs, shiny silk ribbons. And they don't look like artfully posed arrangements but seem to belong quite naturally: a gold-sprayed sea shell next to the fruit bowl in an alcove; a piece of shiny ribbon on the old chest in the hall; a candle on the chimneypiece.

By now, most of the dinner preparations have been completed. The huge sideboard in the kitchen is laden with cakes, biscuits, and chocolate candies.

During the weeks before Christmas Rosamunde Pilcher puts festive touches all over the house. Here the chimneypiece in the drawing room.

"That's when I'm really glad to have a big kitchen," says Rosamunde. "You just put everything down somewhere and then you can forget about it all."

In the afternoon, granddaughter Florence and one of her girlfriends help decorate the tree. Carefully the three of them unwrap Christmas balls, golden

On the day before Christmas, almost all the delicacies have been prepared and are ready on the dresser, the big sideboard in the kitchen.

"I save my pretty Christmas
ornaments and enjoy them
year after year, but something
new is also always added."

angels, and other ornaments, taking
them out of the tissue paper in which
Rosamunde had stored them. At last the
work of art is completed. During the
night Father Christmas will descend
down the chimney, put the presents
under the tree, and fill the stockings that
the children have hung from the end of
their beds.

Christmas Day

Long before the tradition of a decorated pine tree at Christmas was introduced, it was customary to deck the house with mistletoe twigs and holly. It's an old custom for lovers to kiss under the mistletoe, which once was a symbol of magic powers among the Druids and somehow made the transition from the winter-solstice festival of ancient times to the Christian Yuletide celebration. The Christmas tree, on the other hand, has a relatively short history; it was not known in England till the middle of the nineteenth century, when Albert of Saxe-Coborg-Gotha, Queen Victoria's Prince-Consort, brought it there. It was during the 1840s that Prince Albert set up the first tree in Windsor Castle, and soon after that most English families adopted the Christmas tree, usually decorated with small British flags. In the houses of the rich a footman would be assigned to watch the tree, to make sure it did not catch fire, and even today Britons are quite wary of the danger of fire: In England and Scotland only electric Christmas lights are used

On Christmas morning the small children are the first to awake, to turn on the lights and be sure that Father Christmas has remembered to come and fill the stockings at the end of the bed. They are never disappointed, and proceed at once to unpack them, finding a host of small gifts, tiny books and pencils, jokes and whistles, miniature bars of soap and bottles of bath oil.

Father Christmas leaves chocolates, nuts, oranges, and other small presents in the stockings the children hang from the end of their beds on Christmas Eve.

Always at the toe of the stocking is a bag of chocolate pennies wrapped in gold foil, and a juicy, aromatic tangerine.

Since St. Nicholas, together with all other saints, was banished from Protestant Britain hundreds of years ago, this has become the task of Father Christmas, to fill the stockings of children on Christmas Eve. Since he comes dashing down from the North Pole in his reindeer-driven sled, landing always on the roofs of the houses where good children live, he climbs down the chimney to deliver the presents. And this year, besides all the other gifts, Florence and Claudia have received coloured crayons and drawing books, and these pass the time until the grown-ups finally begin to stir.

At last the time has come. Everyone is awake. The log fires are lit. And it is time for tea and coffee, and a light breakfast to save room for all the eating still to come. At ten o'clock, with a certain scramble to be on time, the assembled house party packs into cars, and drives to church, All Saints, Glencarse. After the service there is always a bit of standing around in the cold, greeting other friends, but finally back into the car again, and home, to assemble in the

Little girls need extra-big stockings.

drawing room, open a bottle of champagne, and start in on the holly-wrapped packages piled under the tree.

The Pilcher family prefer to give small, carefully chosen gifts, rather than expensive, lavish presents. "My children and grandchildren often give me little luxury items that I would never buy myself," says Rosamunde. "A special box of soap, a tiny bottle of my favourite scent. Sometimes I ask for a wooden spoon or screwdriver, because that is what I really need. And sometimes they all club together and buy me a piece of china or

Everybody goes for a walk on Christmas afternoon. These pictures from the family album show a white Christmas, which occurs only rarely in this part of Scotland.

Above left, from left to right: Mark Pilcher's girlfriend Jess, Fiona, Mark, and Rosamunde Pilcher. Above right, from left to right: Fiona, Jess, Fiona's husband Will, Penelope Wynn-Williams, and Rosamunde Pilcher. Below, from left to right: Jess, Mark, Fiona, and Rosamunde Pilcher.

53

O come, all ye faithful

1   O come, all ye faithful,

Joyful and triumphant,

O come ye, O come ye to Bethlehem;

Come and behold him,

Born the King of angels:

O come, let us adore him,

O come, let us adore him,

O come, let us adore him, Christ the Lord!

2   God of God,

Light of Light,

Lo, he abhors not the Virgin's womb;

Very God,

Begotten, not created:

3   Sing, choirs of angels,

Sing in exultation

Sing, all ye citizens of heaven above;

Glory to God

In the highest:

4   Yea, Lord, we greet thee,

Born this happy morning,

Jesus, to thee be glory given;

Word of the Father,

Now in flesh appearing:

1   Herbei, o ihr Gläub'gen, fröhlich

triumphieret,

o kommet, o kommet nach Bethlehem!

Sehet das Kindlein uns zum Heil geboren!

O lasset uns anbeten,

o lasset uns anbeten,

o lasset uns anbeten den König!

2   Du König der Ehren, Herrscher der

Heerscharen / verschmäht nicht zu ruhn

in Marien Schoß, / Gott, wahrer Gott von

Ewigkeit geboren.

O lasset uns anbeten, / o lasset uns anbe-

ten, / o lasset uns anbeten den König!

3   Kommt, singet dem Herren, singt,

ihr Engelchöre! / Frohlocket, frohlocket,

ihr Seligen: / «Ehre sei Gott im Himmel

und auf Erden!»

4   Ja, dir, der du heute Mensch für uns

geboren, / Herr Jesu, sei Ehre und Preis

und Ruhm, / dir, fleischgewordenes Wort

des ewgen Vaters!

Text and music by John Fran-
cis Wade, after "Adeste
Fideles," an old Latin hymn.

porcelain dinner plates.'' This year she gives a fountain pen to her husband. The children love pullovers and scarves in brightly coloured cashmere, and the grandchildren all got paperweights made of their initials, or slim leather diaries with their initials embossed in gold. Granddaughter Florence also gets a pair of riding boots, for which she had longed with all her heart.

So, by two o'clock, the drawing room is a rubble of Christmas paper and ribbon, empty champagne glasses and piles of exciting new possessions. Lunch, another light meal, is usually eaten just before the midwinter Scottish sun begins to drop down out of the sky, and so after lunch, everybody is dragooned, like it or not, out of doors for a walk, and if there

is snow on the ground, which sometimes happens, there are snowball fights and a good deal of horseplay.

Dark now, and home again to tea: scones and jam and Christmas cake; tea for the grown-ups and hot chocolate for the children. In their sitting room, the television is switched on, new toys are

Rosamunde and Graham Pilcher enjoy the quiet before the big celebration. Daisy the dachshund, however, is getting impatient.

played with, or new books perused. The men collapse in armchairs with yesterday's newspapers, and the girls repair to the kitchen to start the dinner cooking. The turkey has already been tucked into the oven, and the table laid, so there are quiet moments, time for a leisurely bath, a nap, or just to sit by the fire. Both Graham and Rosamunde relish a moment of peace before the celebration. This is necessary. "It's wonderful to have a large family and a houseful of guests," says Rosamunde, "but sometimes one needs to withdraw for a little to catch one's breath."

The party starts at seven-thirty, when other invited guests appear, all dressed in formal finery, to drink champagne or Scotch and soda before the children make their invasion. The little girls love

Family and guests gather around the fireplace. From left to right: Florence; Claudia, Robin Pilcher's wife Kirsty; Rosemary, a cousin; Rosamunde; Graham; Hugo; Rosamunde Pilcher's girlfriend Sara; Alice and her father Robin.

to dress up, but the boys prefer their open-necked shirts and clean jeans, and it's Christmas so they are allowed to be comfortable.

O little town of Bethlehem

1   O little town of Bethlehem,
How still we see thee lie!
Above thy deep and dreamless sleep
The silent stars go by.
Yet in thy dark streets shineth
The everlasting light;
The hopes and fears of all the years
Are met in thee to-night.

2   O morning stars, together
Proclaim the holy birth,
An praises sing to God the King,
And peace to men on earth;
For Christ is born of Mary;
And, gathered all above,
While mortals sleep, the angels keep
Their watch of wondering love.

3   O holy Child of Bethlehem,
Descend to us, we pray;
Cast out our sin, and enter in,
Be born in us to-day.

We hear the Christmas angels
The great glad tidings tell:
O come to us, abide with us,
Our Lord Emmanuel.

1   O Bethlehem, du kleine Stadt,

wie stille liegst du hier,

du schläfst, und goldne Sternelein ziehn

leise über dir.

Doch in den dunklen Gassen das ewge Licht

heut scheint

für alle, die da traurig sind und die zuvor

geweint.

2   Des Herren heilige Geburt / verkün-

det hell der Stern, / ein ewger Friede sei

beschert / den Menschen nah und fern; /

denn Christus ist geboren, / und Engel hal-

ten Wacht, / dieweil die Menschen schlafen

/ die ganze dunkle Nacht.

3   O heilig Kind von Bethlehem, / in

unsre Herzen komm, / wirf alle unsre

Sünden fort / und mach uns frei und

fromm! / Die Weihnachtsengel singen /

die frohe Botschaft hell: / Komm auch zu

uns und bleib bei uns, / o Herr Immanuel.

Text by Phillips Brooks;
music by Lewis H. Redner.

Dinner is served at eight o'clock, and lasts for at least two hours, ending with the crackers being pulled, and paper hats being donned. After dinner, it's back to the drawing room and games: charades and acting games, guessing games and treasure hunts. Sometimes there is music, all singing to the guitar, or one of the children will perform a special party act. Sometimes, if there has been time to arrange it all and rehearse, there is even a short and fairly disorganized play.

Another English traditional, though not quite harmless Christmas game is snapdragon. Brandy is poured over a bowlful of currants and ignited. The players in turn have to snap up the currants from the flames and eat them.

"I think that's for me." Best girlfriends under the Christmas tree.

While the grown-ups sit by the fireplace, the children unpack their gifts.

The Holiday Feast

The focal point of the traditional sumptuous meal on Christmas Day in England and Scotland is the turkey. Although the bird is called "turkey," it originally came from Mexico, not Turkey. However, it was Levantine merchants who first imported the bird in the sixteenth century, and the English named this strange animal after them. At first the Mexican turkeys looked more like guinea fowl rather than the well-fed Christmas bird of today. But soon several Norfolk farmers began breeding them, and it took only a few decades for the bird to attain its present impressive size. In the seventeenth century, English settlers took some prime specimens along when they emigrated to America, where the turkey is on everyone's Thanksgiving table till today.

Not quite so far, but almost equally arduous, was transporting the turkeys from Norfolk to the London Christmas market. Soon after the harvest, as early as the end of August, the dealers began the long trek with the animals. The roads were unpaved and muddy, and often the birds would actually get stuck in the muck, so many of the traders supplied them with footwear by wrapping sackcloth or leather strips around their feet. There's an anecdote that has come down to us about a race between a flock of turkeys and a flock of geese, won by the geese. Although the geese were slower waddling along, they were able to eat while in motion, which gave them a big advantage.

The turkey—the pièce de résistance of a Scottish Christmas dinner.

Because of these problems, the turkey wasn't exactly inexpensive, and even at Christmastime the only people who could afford one were those who were able to spend more on one holiday dinner than what many others might earn all year. Not till the end of the nineteenth century, when improved roads and better storage methods had been devised, did prices become more affordable. But even today the turkey is more than just one holiday meal. Almost just as important are the trimmings: the filling, sauces, and side dishes. Each family has its own secret recipe, and it is generally expected that a fifteen-pound turkey plus trimmings will yield leftovers for several days. Turkey sandwiches with gravy are the traditional meal for the day after Christmas.

Roast Turkey

1 oven-ready turkey (for 6–8 people; ca. 12–15 lbs./5–6 kg.)

7 oz./250 g. bacon strips

4 tablespoons/50 g. butter

Fill turkey (see filling recipes), coat with butter, and lay bacon strips across breast. Add salt and pepper and wrap in aluminum foil. Roast about 3 hours in a preheated 400-degree F. oven (the exact time should come to about 15 minutes per pound, including the filling.) Open the foil cover and roast another hour till crips, basting with drippings from time to time. When done, let the turkey rest at least 30 minutes in a warm place before carving.

Sage-and-Onion Stuffing

1 lb./500 g. onions

20 fresh sage leaves or 2 heaped
    teaspoons dried sage

about ¾ lb./400 g. white bread or rolls

4 oz./100 g. melted butter

2 eggs, lightly beaten

salt and pepper

Bring onions to boil in a little water and simmer about 10 minutes in a covered saucepan. Drain water. If fresh sage is used, blanch in hot water, drain and mince. Mince cooked onions. Combine onions, sage, breadcrumbs, butter, and eggs. Season with salt and pepper.

Chestnut Stuffing

1½ lbs./700 g. chestnuts

1 goose liver, finely minced

5 oz./125 g. melted butter

salt and pepper

Cut a cross into each chestnut, cover with water and simmer about 20 minutes. Do not drain water. Take chestnuts out of water one at a time and peel (both outer hard shell and inner fine skin). Finely mince half of the chestnuts; leave rest whole. Mix with the liver and butter and season with salt and pepper.

Spicy Red Cabbage

1 head of red cabbage

4 tablespoons/50 g. butter

4 tart apples

2 tablespoons vinegar

6 oz./200 g. bacon strips

2 large onions

2 teaspoons brown sugar

salt and pepper

Cut cabbage into quarters, remove stalk and cut cabbage into fine strips. Fry bacon in a little butter till crisp, remove and keep warm. Add rest of butter and onions to saucepan and gently sauté onions till golden. Peel and core apples and cut into chunks. Stack cabbage, apples, onions, and bacon in a heavy saucepan, season each layer with salt, pepper, a little sugar, and vinegar. Add a cup of hot water, sprinkle with a little sugar and dot with butter. Cover tightly and simmer on low heat for about 45 minutes.

Brussels Sprouts with Chestnuts

1 lb./500 g. Brussels sprouts

½ lb./250 g. chestnuts

4 tablespoons/50 g. butter

5 oz./150 ml. chicken broth

salt and pepper

Cut a cross into each chestnut, cover with water and bring to boil. Simmer about 5 minutes, till shells burst. Take saucepan off fire but do not drain. One by one, take chestnuts out of hot water and peel (both outer shell and inner fine skin).

Clean Brussels sprouts. Melt butter in a heavy saucepan, add chestnuts, and sauté a few minutes. Add chicken broth, cover saucepan and simmer about 20 minutes. Add Brussels sprouts and more broth if vegetables are not covered. Season with salt and pepper and let simmer another 10 minutes. Drain, check seasonings and serve.

Bread Sauce

7 oz./200 ml. milk

1 onion

3 slices white bread

1 tablespoon butter

1 bay leaf

salt and pepper

Mince onion and sauté in butter until transparent. Dice bread or crumble in mixer, add to onions together with milk. Add bay leaf, season with salt and pepper, and simmer on low heat for about 30 minutes. Remove bay leaf and add a piece of cold butter. Serve warm with turkey.

Cranberry Sauce

1 lb./450 g. cranberries (fresh or frozen)

10 oz. (1¼ cups)/300 ml. water

1½ cups/350 g. sugar

juice of half an orange

splash of red wine (optional)

Pick over cranberries. Add sugar to water and dissolve on low heat. Add cranberries, bring to boil. Remove from fire and add orange juice and red wine, if desired. Simmer everything about 10 minutes, until cranberries are soft. Drain, reserving liquid. Boil down liquid until slightly thickened. Add berries, let cool and serve with turkey.

Ice-Cream-Filled Oranges

6 oranges

1 pint (2 cups)/500 ml.
frozen orange juice

1 pint/500 ml. vanilla
ice-cream

Cut a lid off the top of the oranges. Carefully remove orange flesh and reserve for another use. Melt ice-cream and frozen orange juice and stir together. Refreeze. Fill the still-creamy mixture into the oranges, cover with lids and put into freezer. Remove from freezer about 30 minutes before oranges are served. If desired, decorate with any pretty green leaves, such as bay leaves.

The last course of the Christmas feast is always the Christmas pudding. Served on a large platter, it is decorated with holly twigs and flambéed. The preparation is part of the ritual of the pudding.

Traditionally it is made on the fifth Sunday before Christmas. The whole family assembles in the kitchen, and everyone takes a turn at stirring it. In remembrance of the journey of the Three Wise Men, the pudding is stirred from east to west while everyone makes a wish. Whatever is wished for is a secret, but it is pretty certain that it will come true during the coming year—especially for the lucky one who finds the silver coin, hidden in the pudding during its preparation, on Christmas Day.

Christmas Pudding

½ cup/75 g. flour

3 oz./75 g. chopped suet or lard

3 oz./75 g. crumbed bread or rolls

3 oz./75 g. currants

5 oz./120 g. golden raisins

5 oz./120 g. dark raisins

3 oz./75 g. brown sugar

dash each of ground cloves, paprika, cinnamon, and nutmeg

2 oz./50 g. candied orange peel or citron, chopped

2 oz./50 g. candied cherries, chopped

1 small carrot, grated

1/2 small apple, peeled and grated

2 eggs, slightly beaten

grated rind and juice of 1/2 orange and 1/2 lemon

1/2 cup/100 ml. dark beer (Guinness or stout)

In a large bowl stir together flour, suet or lard, breadcrumbs, candied fruits, sugar, salt, spices, lemon- and orange peels, carrot, and apple. Beat together eggs, lemon- and orange juice, and beer, add to dry ingredients and stir everything together to make a thick, viscous batter. If necessary, add some more beer. Pour the batter into a 1 1/2-quart

greased pudding mold with a tightly fitting lid and steam 7 hours. (Set pudding on a trivet in a heavy kettle with 1 inch of boiling water. Keep adding more water as it evaporates.) When done, remove pudding mold and store in a cool place for at least six weeks. Before serving, reheat for three hours before unmoulding onto a platter. Decorate with holly twigs. Pour a small glass of cognac over the pudding and ignite and serve flambéed.

Brandy Butter

4 oz./125 g. butter

2 teaspoons sugar

4 teaspoons brandy

Cream together butter and sugar. Add brandy drop by drop, beating constantly, until a creamy sauce is formed.

After the dessert, cheese may be served. Rosamunde herself prefers a piece of Stilton to any sweet dish, but generally the cheese platter is not fully appreciated till the day after Christmas. Although the selection of English cheeses is not as varied nor as well-known as French cheeses, they are every bit as flavoursome as their Gallic counterparts. This is especially true of the Stilton, a superb blue cheese that has been known since the eighteenth century and is traditionally served with celery sticks and port wine.

The oldest English cheese is the Cheshire, which derives its name from the county Cheshire in western England and is supposed to date back to Roman times. By now, it is available world-wide, although it is sometimes sold under the name "Chester" in Europe.

The favourite cheese among Britons is the cheddar, named after the town by that name in Somerset County. Originally derived from sheep's milk, which was plentiful in southern England, it is today made from cow's milk and is available in different degrees of ripeness: mild cheddar ripens in three months, whereas the sharp, mature cheddar is stored for up to two years before it is sold.

Besides these three most popular cheeses, British grocery stores offer a large selection of other kinds: Lancashire, Double Gloucester, Caerphilly, and the Irish Cashel Blue. They are usually served with wafer-thin crackers and pickle, a kind of pungent chutney made from vegetables, apples, and spices.

On Christmas Day, there is little left to do for the mistress of the house. The

Dinner is served: turkey with trimmings, ice-cream-filled oranges, Christmas pudding, cheese tray. Australian white wine and French burgundy

dinner was prepared the day before. Rosamunde's girlfriend Sara takes care of the turkey and trimmings, and which have all been made and only need to be reheated on the Aga shortly before dinner. Rosamunde has already set the table in the dining room the evening before. She likes to combine old family heirloom pieces, like the silver service, with articles of modern design, such as, for instance, simple glass plates for bread and butter. The table is decorated with candles and flowers. Serving dishes and platters are not put on the dining table, but are kept on the sideboard.

At eight o'clock family and guests sit down to dinner, which often lasts till late at night. Towards the end, when the plum pudding is served, the Christmas crackers are exploded, everybody dons a colourful paper hat and maybe even a cardboard nose and, among much cheering and laughter, the jokes and puns from the crackers are read out loud.

Christmas crackers have been part of British Christmas tradition since the middle of the nineteenth century. They were invented by the English confectionery manufacturer Tom Smith, whose company exists to this day. A trip to France gave him the idea to sell small sweets wrapped in silk paper—that's how the bonbon was introduced in Britain. Since the sale of the sweets, which

There's a Christmas cracker
next to every plate.

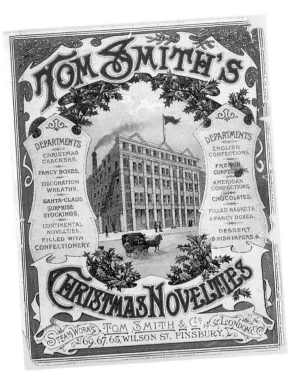

Christmas crackers are the invention of the English sweets manufacturer Tom Smith, whose company exists to this day.

were mostly bought as Christmas presents, sank drastically after the holiday season, Smith, getting the inspiration from wedding cakes, began to add little notes with declarations of love. In 1847, Tom Smith thought up the Christmas cracker, which explodes with a bang when pulled apart. At first the crackers only contained notes with Christmas wishes or general wise sayings. Later on, colourful cardboard hats and -noses were introduced, and instead of wise sayings the crackers today contain puns and particularly silly jokes, which the party members read out loud to one another.

Crackers and cardboard hats remind us of the fireworks and party hats people don on New Year's Eve, a custom not known in Great Britain. But whether observed at Christmas or on New Year's Eve, the historical origin of the noise-making and dressing-up is the same. It goes back to the Romans, who celebrated the Saturnalia during the winter solstice, a festival lasting several days, with banquets, games, and fancy dress, to honour the god Saturn and to welcome back the return of the sunlight.

The family is gathered around the dinner-table for the big feast. From left to right: Florence, Claudia, Alice, Hugo, Rosamunde, Robin, Sara, Kirsty, Rosemary (partially obscured), Graham. "Christmas should be a warm, cosy holiday above all. Guests as well as hosts should feel comfortable and at ease and enjoy the time they spend together."

Graham and Rosamunde Pilcher.

Above left: Alice; above right:
Florence. Below left: Hugo;
below right: Kirsty and Rosemary.

Miss Cameron at Christmas

The little town, which was called Kilmoran, had many faces, and all of them, to Miss Cameron, were beautiful. In spring, the waters of the firth were blown blue as indigo; inland the fields were filled with lambs, and cottage gardens danced with daffodils. The summer brought the visitors; family parties camping on the beach, swimming in the shallow waves, the ice-cream van parked by the breakwater, the old man with his donkey giving rides to the children. And then, around the middle of September, the visitors disappeared, the holiday houses were closed up, their shuttered windows staring blank-eyed across the water to the hills on the distant shore. The countryside hummed with combine harvesters, and as the leaves began to flutter from the trees and the stormy autumn tides brought the sea right up to the rim of the wall below Miss Cameron's garden, the first of the wild geese flew in from the north. After the geese, she always felt it was winter.

And perhaps, thought Miss Cameron privately, that was the most beautiful time of all. Her house faced south across the firth, and although she often woke to darkness and wind and the battering of rain, sometimes the sky was clear and cloudless, and on such mornings she would lie in her bed and watch the red sun edge its way over the horizon and flood her bedroom with rosy light. It winked on the brass rail of her bed and was reflected in the mirror over the dressing-table.

Now, it was the twenty-fourth of December, and just such a morning. Christmas tomorrow. She was alone, and she would spend tomorrow alone. She did not mind. She and her house would keep each other company. She got up and went to close the window. There was an icing of snow on the distant Lammermuirs and a gull sat on the wall at the end of the garden, screaming over a piece of rotton fish. Suddenly it spread its wings and took off. The sunlight caught the spread of white feathers and transformed the gull into a magic pink bird, so beautiful that Miss Cameron's heart lifted in pleasure and excitement. She watched the gull's flight until it dipped out of sight, then turned to find her slippers and go downstairs to put on a kettle for her cup of tea.

Miss Cameron was fifty-eight. Until two years ago she had lived in Edinburgh, in the tall, cold, north-facing house where she had been born and brought up.

She had been an only child, the daughter of parents so much older than herself that by the time she was twenty, they were already well on the road to old age. This made leaving home and making a life for herself, if not impossible, then difficult. Somehow, she achieved a sort of compromise. She got herself to University, but it was Edinburgh University, and she lived at home. After that, she had taken a teaching job, but that, too, had been in a local school, and by the time she was thirty, there could be no question of abandoning the two old people who—unbelievably, Miss Cameron often thought—were responsible for her very existence.

When she was forty, her mother, who had never been very robust, had a little heart attack, lay feebly in her bed for a month or so, and then died. After the funeral, Miss Cameron and her father returned to the tall and gloomy house. He went upstairs to sit morosely by the fire, and she went down to the kitchen and made him a cup of tea. The kitchen was in the basement, and the window had bars on it, to discourage possible intruders. Miss Cameron, waiting for the kettle to boil, looked out through the bars to the small stone area beyond. She had tried to grow geraniums there, but they had all died, and now there was nothing to be seen but a stubborn sprout of willow herb. The bars made the kitchen feel like a prison. She had never thought this before, but she thought it now, and knew that it was true. She would never get away.

Her father lived on for another fifteen years, and she went on teaching until he became too frail to leave, even for a day. So she dutifully retired from her job, where she had been not exactly happy, but at least fulfilled, and stayed at home, to devote her time to what remained of her father's life. She had little money of her own, and supposed that the old man had as little as herself, so frugal was the housekeeping allowance, so cautious was he with things like coal and central heating and even the most modest forms of enjoyment.

He owned an old car, which Miss Cameron could drive, and on warm days she used sometimes to bundle him into this, and he would sit beside her, in his grey tweed suit and the black hat that made him look like an undertaker, while she drove him to the seaside or the country, or even to Holyrood Park, where he could take a little stumbling walk, or sit in the sun beneath the grassy slopes of Arthur's Seat. But then the price of petrol rocketed, and without consulting his daughter, Mr. Cameron sold the car, and she did not have enough money of her own to buy another.

She had a friend, Dorothy Laurie, with whom she had been at University. Dorothy had married—as Miss Cameron had not—a young doctor, who was now an eminently successful neurologist, and with whose cooperation she had produced a family of satisfactory children, now all grown up. Dorothy was perpetually indignant about Miss Cameron's situation. She felt, and said, that Miss Cameron's parents had been selfish and thoughtless, and that the old man was getting worse as he was getting older. When the car was sold, she blew her top.

"It's ridiculous," she said, over tea in her sunny, flower-filled drawing room. Miss Cameron had prevailed upon her daily help to stay over for the afternoon to give Mr. Cameron his tea, and make sure that he didn't fall down the stairs on his way to the lavatory. "He can't be as penurious as all that. Surely he can afford to run a car, for your sake, if not for his own?"

Miss Cameron did not like to point out that he had never thought of any person except himself. She said, "I don't know."

"Then you should find out. Speak to his accountant. Or his lawyer."

"Dorothy, I couldn't. It would be so disloyal."

Dorothy made a sound which sounded like "Pshaw" and which is what people used to say in old-fashioned novels.

"I don't want to upset him," Miss Cameron went on.

"Do him good to be upset. If he'd been upset once or twice in his life, he wouldn't be such a selfish old . . ." She bit back what she had been going to say and substituted ". . . man, now."

"He's lonely."

"Of course he's lonely. Selfish people are always lonely. That's nobody's fault but his own. For years, he's sat in a chair and felt sorry for himself."

It was too true to argue with. "Oh, well," said Miss Cameron feebly, "it can't be helped. He's nearly ninety now. It's too late to start trying to change him."

"Yes, but it's not too late to change you. You mustn't let yourself grow old with him. You must keep some part of life for yourself."

He died at last, painlessly and peacefully, falling asleep after a quiet evening and an excellent dinner cooked for him by his daughter, and never waking again. Miss Cameron was glad for him that the end had come so quietly. There was a funeral and a surprising number of people attended it. A day or so later, Miss Cameron was summoned to her father's lawyer's office. She went, in a black hat and a state of nervous apprehension. But as it happened, nothing turned out as she had thought it would. Mr. Cameron, the canny old Scot that he was, had played his cards very close to his chest. The penny-pinching, the austerity of years, had been one huge, magnificent bluff. He left in his will, to his daughter, his house, his worldly possessions, and more money than she had ever dreamt of. Polite, and outwardly composed as ever, she left the lawyer's office and stepped out into the sunlight of Charlotte Square. There was a flag flying high over the ramparts of the castle and the air was cold and fresh. She walked down to Jenners and had a cup of coffee, and then she went to see Dorothy.

Dorothy, on hearing the news, was characteristically torn between fury at old Mr. Cameron's meanness and duplicity and delight in her friend's good fortune. "You can buy a car," she told her. "You can travel. You can have a fur coat, go on cruises. Anything. What are you going to do? What are you going to do with the rest of your life?"

"Well," said Miss Cameron cautiously, "I will buy myself a little car." The idea of being free, mobile, with no person but herself to consider, took a bit of getting used to.

"And travel?"

But Miss Cameron had no great desire for travel, except that one day she would like to go to Oberammergau and see the Passion Play. And she didn't want to go on cruises. She really wanted only one thing. Had wanted only one thing in her life. And now she could have it.

She said, "I shall sell the Edinburgh house. And I shall buy another."

"Where?"

She knew exactly where. Kilmoran. She had gone there for a summer when she was ten, invited by the kindly parents of a school friend. It had been a holiday of such happiness that Miss Cameron had never forgotten it.

She said, "I shall go and live in Kilmoran."

"Kilmoran? But that's only just across the firth . . ."

Miss Cameron smiled at her. It was a smile that Dorothy had never seen before, and it silenced her. "That is where I shall buy a house."

And so she did. A house in a terrace, facing out over the sea. From the back, from the north, its aspect was both plain and dull, with square windows and a front door that led straight off the pavement. But inside, it was beautiful, a Georgian house in miniature, with a slate-flagged hallway and a curving staircase rising to the upper floor. The sitting-room was upstairs, with a bay window, and in front of the house was a square garden, walled in from the sea winds. There was a tall gate in the wall, and if you opened this, a flight of stone steps led down the sea-wall to the beach. In summer, children ran along the top of the sea-wall and screamed and shouted at each other, but Miss Cameron minded this noise no more than she minded the noise of the waves, or the gulls, or the eternal winds.

There was much to be done to the house and much to be spent on it, but with a certain mouse-like courage, she both did and spent. Central heating was installed, and double glazing. The kitchen was rebuilt, with pine cupboards, and new pale-green bathroom fixtures took the place of the old white chipped ones.

The prettiest and smallest articles of furniture were weeded out of the old Edinburgh house and transported, in an immense van, to Kilmoran, along with the china, the silver, the familiar pictures. But she bought new carpets and curtains, and had all the walls repapered and the woodwork painted a shining white.

As for the garden—she had never had a garden before. Now she bought books and studied them in bed at night, and she planted escallonia and veronica and thyme and sea-lavender, and bought a little lawnmower and cut the ragged, turfy grass herself.

It was through her garden that she met, inevitably, her neighbours. On the right-hand side lived the Mitchells, an elderly retired couple. They chatted over the garden wall, and one day Mrs. Mitchell invited Miss Cameron for supper and a game of bridge. Cautiously, they became Miss Cameron's friends, but they were old-fashioned and formal people, and did not suggest that Miss Cameron call them by their Christian names, and she was too reserved to suggest the idea herself. Thinking about it, she realized that now the only person who called her by her Christian name was Dorothy. It was sad when people stopped realizing that you had a Christian name. It meant that you were growing old.

However, the neighbours on the left-hand side of Miss Cameron's house were a different kettle of fish altogether. In the first place, they did not live permanently in their house, but used it only at weekends and for holidays.

"They're called Ashley," Mrs. Mitchell had volunteered over the supper table, when Miss Cameron had made one or two discreet inquiries about the closed and shuttered house on the other side of her garden. "He's an architect with a practice in Edinburgh. I'm surprised you've not heard of him, living there all your life, as you have. Ambrose Ashley. He married a girl much younger than himself . . . she was a painter, I think . . . and they have a daughter. She seems a nice little girl . . . Now have a little more quiche, Miss Cameron, or perhaps some salad?"

It was Easter when the Ashleys appeared. Good Friday was cold and bright, and when Miss Cameron went out into her garden, she heard the voices from over the wall, and she looked at the house and saw the shutters down and the windows open. A pink curtain fluttered in the breeze. Then a girl appeared at the upstairs window, and she and Miss Cameron, for a second, gazed into each other's faces. Miss Cameron was embarrassed. She turned and hurried indoors. How terrible if they thought she was prying.

But later in the day, while she was weeding, she heard her name being called, and there was the same girl, looking at her over the top of the wall. She had a round and freckled face, dark brown eyes, and reddish hair, abundant and thick and wind-blown.

Miss Cameron got up off her knees and crossed the lawn, pulling off her gardening gloves.

"I'm Frances Ashley . . ." Over the wall, they shook hands. Close to, Miss Cameron realized that she was not as young as she had at first appeared. There were lines around her eyes and mouth, and perhaps that blaze of hair wasn't entirely natural, but her expression was so open, and she gave off such an aura of vitality, that Miss Cameron lost some of her shyness, and felt, almost at once, at ease.

The dark eyes travelled over Miss Cameron's garden. "Goodness, how hard you must have worked. You've made it all so neat and pretty. Are you doing anything on Sunday? Easter Sunday? Because we're having a barbecue in the garden, provided it doesn't pour with rain. Do come, if you don't mind joining in a picnic."

"Oh. How kind." Miss Cameron had never been invited to a barbecue. "I . . . think I'd like to come very much."

"About a quarter to one. You can come by the sea-wall."

"I shall look forward to that very much."

During the next couple of days, she realized that life with the Ashleys in residence next door was very different from life without them. For one thing,

there was much more noise, but it was a pleasant noise. Voices calling and laughter and music that floated out through the open windows. Miss Cameron, steeling herself for "hard rock," or whatever it was called, recognized Vivaldi and was filled with pleasure. She caught glimpses of the remainder of the little family. The father, very tall and thin and distinguished, with a head of silver hair, and the daughter, who was as red-headed as her mother and had legs that looked endless in faded jeans. They had friends to stay as well (Miss Cameron wondered how they were packing them all in), and in the afternoons they would all surge down the garden and invade the beach, playing ridiculous ball games, the red-headed mother and daughter looking like sisters as they raced, barefooted, across the sands.

Easter Sunday dawned bright and sunny, although the wind was keen and cold and there was still a scrap of snow to be seen, clinging to the crest of the Lammermuirs across the water. Miss Cameron went to church, then came home to change out of her Sunday coat and skirt and to put on something more suitable for a picnic. She had never owned a pair of trousers, but she found a comfortable skirt, a warm sweater, and a windproof anorak, then locked her front door and went out of the house, through the garden, along the sea-wall, and in through the gate of the Ashleys's garden. Smoke was blowing from the newly lighted barbecue and the little lawn was already crowded with people of every age, some sitting on garden chairs or camped on rugs. Everybody seemed very jolly and as though they all knew one another very well, and for a second Miss Cameron was overcome with shyness and wished that she hadn't come. But then Ambrose Ashley materialized at her side, towering over her and holding a toasting fork with a burnt sausage skewered to its end.

"Miss Cameron. How splendid to meet you. And how good of you to come. Happy Easter. Now come and meet everybody. Frances! Here's Miss Cameron. We've invited the Mitchells, too, but they haven't arrived yet. Frances, how do we stop the fire from smoking? I can't give this sausage to anyone but a dog."

Frances laughed. "Then find a dog and give it to him, and then start again . . ." And suddenly Miss Cameron was laughing too, because he did look marvellously comic, with his straight face and his burnt sausage. Then somebody found her a chair and somebody else gave her a tumbler of wine. She was about to tell this person who she was and where she lived when she was interrupted by a plateful of food being handed to her. She looked up and into the face of the Ashley daughter. The dark eyes were her mother's, but the smile was her father's engaging grin. She could not have been more than twelve, but Miss Cameron, who had watched countless girls grow up during her years of teaching, knew at once that this child was going to be a beauty.

"Would you like something to eat?"

"I'd love something to eat." She looked about her for somewhere to put her glass, then set it on the grass. She took the plate, the paper napkin, the knife and fork. "Thank you. I don't think I know your name?"

"I'm Bryony. I hope you like steaks pink in the middle, because that's what this one is."

"Delicious," said Miss Cameron, who liked her steaks very well done.

"And there's butter on the baked potato. I put it there so that you wouldn't have to get up." She smiled and moved away, back to help her mother.

Miss Cameron, trying to organize her knife and fork, turned back to her neighbour. "What a pretty child."

"Yes, she's a darling. Now I'm going to get you another glass of wine, and then you must go on telling me all about the fascinating house."

It was a wonderful party and did not finish until six. When it was time to go, the tide was so high that Miss Cameron did not relish walking along the sea-wall, and so returned to her own house the conventional way, via front doors and the pavement. Ambrose Ashley came with her. When she had opened her door, she turned to thank him.

"Such a lovely party. I did enjoy it. I feel quite Bohemian, drinking all that wine in the middle of the day. And I hope, when you next come, you will all come and have a meal with me. Luncheon, perhaps."

"We'd love it, but we won't be coming back for a bit. I've got a teaching job at a university in Texas. We're going out in July, having a bit of a holiday first, and then I start work in the fall. It's a sort of sabbatical. Byrony's coming too. She'll have to go to school in the States, but we don't want to leave her behind."

"What a marvellous experience for you all!" He smiled down at her, and she said, with truth, "You will be missed."

The seasons passed. Spring turned to summer, to autumn, to winter. There were storms and the Ashleys's escallonia was blown from the wall, so Miss Cameron took herself next door with garden wire and cutters and tied it up. It was Easter again, it was summer, but still the Ashleys did not reappear. It was not until the end of August that they came back. Miss Cameron had been shopping and changing her library book. She came round the corner at the end of the street and saw their car parked by their door, and her heart gave a ridiculous leap. She let herself into her house, put her basket onto the kitchen table, and went straight out into the garden. And there, over the wall, was Mr. Ashley, trying to cut down the ragged, overgrown grass with a scythe. He looked up and saw her, and stopped in the middle of a sweep. "Miss Cameron." He laid down the scythe and came over to shake her hand.

"You're back." She could scarcely contain her pleasure.

"Yes. We stayed longer than we had intended. We made so many friends and there was so much to see, and so much to do. It was a wonderful experience for all of us. But now we're back in Edinburgh, and I'm back in harness."

"How long are you staying here?"

"Just a couple of nights, I'm afraid. It's going to take me all that time to get rid of the grass . . ."

But Miss Cameron's attention had wandered. A movement from the house caught her eye. The door opened and Frances Ashley came out, and down the steps towards them. After a second's hesitation, Miss Cameron smiled, and said, "Welcome back. I'm so pleased to see you both again."

She hoped so much that they had not noticed the hesitation. She would not for all the world have wanted them even to guess at her shock and astonishment. For Frances Ashley had returned from America marvellously, obviously, pregnant.

*   *   *

"She's having another baby," said Mrs. Mitchell. "After all this time. She's having another baby."

"Well, there's no reason why she shouldn't have another baby," said Miss Cameron faintly. "I mean, if she wants to."

"But Bryony must be fourteen."

"That doesn't matter."

"No, I know it doesn't matter . . . it's just . . . well, rather unusual."

The two ladies were silent for a moment, agreeing on this.

After a little, "It's not," said Mrs. Mitchell delicately, "as though she was as young as she used to be."

"She looks very young," said Miss Cameron.

"Yes, she does look young, but she must be thirty-eight at least. I mean, I know that is young, when you're getting on in years like we are. But it's not young to have a baby."

Miss Cameron had not realized that Mrs. Ashley was thirty-eight. Sometimes, when she was out on the sands with her leggy daughter, they looked the same age. She said, "I'm sure it will be all right," but even to herself, she didn't sound sure.

"Yes, of course," said Mrs. Mitchell. They met each other's eyes, and then, quickly, both looked away.

*   *   *

And now it was midwinter, and Christmas again, and Miss Cameron was alone. If the Mitchells had been here, she might have asked them over for lunch tomorrow, but they had taken themselves off to spend Christmas in Dorset with a married daughter. So, their house stood empty. On the other hand, the Ashleys's house was occupied. They had arrived from Edinburgh a day or two ago, but Miss Cameron had not spoken to them. She felt that she should, but for some obscure reason it was more difficult to make contact in the wintertime. There could be no casual chat over the garden wall when people stayed indoors with fires lighted and curtains drawn. And she was too diffident to find some reason for contact and go knocking at their door. If she had known them better, she would have bought them Christmas presents, but if they then had nothing for her, it could be embarrassing. As well, there was the complication of Mrs. Ashley's pregnancy. Yesterday Miss Cameron had spied her, hanging out a line of washing, and it appeared as if the baby might arrive at any moment.

In the afternoon Mrs. Ashley and Bryony set out for a walk across the beach. They went slowly, not running and racing as they usually did. Mrs. Ashley wore wellingtons and trod tiredly, heavily, as though weighed down not simply by the bulk of the baby, but by all the anxieties of the world. Even the bounce seemed to have gone from her russet hair. Bryony slowed her pace to match her mother's, and when they returned from their little excursion, she had her hand under her mother's elbow, helping her along.

I mustn't think about them, Miss Cameron told herself briskly. I mustn't

turn into the sort of meddling old lady who watches the neighbours and makes up stories about them. It is nothing to do with me.

Christmas Eve. Determined to be festive, Miss Cameron arranged her cards on the mantelpiece and filled a bowl with holly; brought in logs and cleaned the house, and in the afternoon went for a long walk across the beach. By the time she got home, it was dark, a strange, cloudy evening with a blustery wind

blowing from the west. She drew the curtains and made tea. She was just sitting down to this, her knees close to the blazing fire, when the telephone rang. She got up and went to answer it, and was amazed to hear a man's voice. It was Ambrose Ashley from next door.

He said, "You're there."

"Of course."

"I'm coming round."

He rang off. An instant later her front door bell pealed and she went to answer it. He stood on the pavement, looking ashen, fleshless as a skeleton.

She said at once, "What's wrong?"

"I have to take Frances to Edinburgh, to the hospital."

"Has the baby started?"

"I don't know. But she's been feeling unwell for a day or two. I'm scared. I've rung our doctor, and he says to bring her in right away."

"What can I do to help?"

"That's why I'm here. Could you come across and stay with Bryony? She wants to come with us, but I'd rather not take her and I don't want to leave her on her own."

"Of course." Despite her anxiety, a warmth filled Miss Cameron. They needed her help. They had come to her. "But I think it would be better if she came to me. It might be easier for her."

"You're an angel."

He went back to his own house. A moment later he emerged, with his arm around his wife. They crossed the pavement, and he gently eased her into the car. Bryony followed with her mother's suitcase. She wore her jeans and a thick white pullover, and as she leaned into the car to hug her mother and give her a kiss, Miss Cameron felt a lump come into her throat. Fourteen, she knew of old, could be an impossible age. Old enough to understand, but not old enough to be of practical help. She had a mental picture of Bryony and her mother running off across the sands together, and her heart bled for the child.

The car doors were shut. Mr. Ashley gave his daughter a quick kiss. "I'll call you," he told them both, and then got behind the driving wheel. Minutes later, the car had gone, the red rear lights swallowed into the darkness. Miss Cameron and Bryony were left there, on the pavement, in the dark wind.

Bryony had grown. She was now nearly as tall as Miss Cameron, and it was she who spoke first. "Do you mind me coming through to be with you?" Her voice was controlled and cool.

Miss Cameron decided to follow her example. "Not at all," she told her.

"I'll just lock up the house and put a guard on the fire."

"You do that. I'll be waiting for you."

When she came, Miss Cameron had put more logs on the fire, made a fresh pot of tea, found another cup and saucer, and a packet of chocolate biscuits. Bryony sat on the hearthrug with her thin knees drawn up to her chin, and held her teacup with her long fingers wrapped about it, as though hungry for warmth.

Miss Cameron said, "You must try not to worry. I'm sure everything will be all right."

Bryony said, "She didn't really want this baby. When it started, when we were in America, she said that she was too old for little babies. But then she got used to the idea and got quite excited about it, and we bought clothes in New York and things like that. But the last month, it's all changed again. She seems so tired, and . . . frightened, almost."

"I've never had a baby," said Miss Cameron, "so I don't know how people feel. But I imagine it is rather an emotional time. And you can't help how you feel. It's no good other people telling you not to be depressed."

"She says she's too old. She's nearly forty."

"My mother was forty before I was born, and I was her first and only child. And there's nothing wrong with me and there was nothing wrong with my mother."

Bryony looked up, her attention caught by this revelation. "Was she really? Did you mind, about her being so old?"

Miss Cameron decided that this was one time when the whole truth went out the window. "No, not at all. And for your baby it will be different, because you'll be there. I can't think of anything nicer than having a sister fourteen years older than oneself. Just like having the very best sort of aunt."

"The awful thing is," said Bryony, "I wouldn't mind so much if something happened to the baby. But I couldn't bear anything to happen to my mother."

Miss Cameron leaned forward and gave her a pat on the shoulder. "It won't. Don't think about it. The doctors will take every care of her." It seemed time to try to talk about something else. "Now. It's Christmas Eve. There are carols on television. Would you like to listen to them?"

"No, if you don't awfully mind. I don't want to think about Christmas, and I don't want to watch television."

"Then what would you like to do?"

"I think I'd just like to talk."

Miss Cameron's heart sank. "Talk. What shall we talk about?"

"Perhaps we could talk about you."

"Me?" Despite herself she had to laugh. "My goodness, what a boring subject. An old maiden lady, practically in her dotage!"

"How old are you?" asked Bryony with such simplicity that Miss Cameron told her. "But fifty-eight's not old! That's only a year or two older than my father and he's young. At least, I always think he is."

"I'm afraid I'm still not very interesting."

"I think everybody's interesting. And do you know what my mother said when she first saw you? She said you had a beautiful face and that she would like to draw you. So how's that for a compliment?"

Miss Cameron flushed with pleasure. "Well, that's very gratifying . . ."

"So tell me about you. Why did you buy this little house? Why did you come *here?*"

And so Miss Cameron, normally so reserved and silent, began painfully to talk. She told Bryony about that first holiday in Kilmoran, before the war, when the world was young and innocent and you could buy an ice-cream cone for a penny. She told Bryony about her parents, her childhood, the old, tall house in

Edinburgh. She told her about University, and how she had met her friend Dorothy, and all at once this unaccustomed flood of reminiscence was no longer an ordeal, but a kind of relief. It was pleasant to remember the old-fashioned school where she had taught for so many years, and she was able to speak dispassionately about those last bleak times before her father finally died.

Bryony listened avidly, with as much interest as if Miss Cameron were telling her of some amazing personal adventure. And when she got to the bit about old Mr. Cameron's will, and being left so comfortably off, Bryony could not contain herself.

"Oh, how marvellous. It's just like a fairy story. It's just such a terrible pity there isn't a good-looking, white-haired prince to turn up and claim your hand in marriage."

Miss Cameron laughed. "I'm a little old for that kind of thing."

"What a pity you didn't marry. You'd have been a marvellous sort of mother. Or even if you'd had sisters and brothers and then you could have been the marvellous sort of aunt!" She looked around the little sitting-room with satisfaction. "It's just exactly right for you, isn't it? This house must have been waiting for you, knowing that you were going to come and live here."

"That's a fatalistic sort of attitude."

"Yes, but a positive one. I'm terribly fatalistic about everything."

"You mustn't be too fatalistic. God helps those who help themselves."

"Yes," said Bryony. "Yes, I suppose so."

They fell silent. A log broke and collapsed into the fire, and as Miss Cameron leaned forward to replace it, the clock on the mantelpiece chimed half past seven. They were both astonished to realize that it was so late, and Bryony at once remembered her mother.

"I wonder what's happening?"

"Your father will ring the moment he has anything to tell us. And meantime, I think we should wash up these tea-things and decide what we're going to have for supper. What would you like?"

"My most favourite would be tinned tomato soup and bacon and eggs."

"That would be my most favourite, too. Let's go and get it."

The telephone call did not come through until half past nine. Mrs. Ashley was in labour. There was no saying how long it would be, but Mr. Ashley intended staying at the hospital.

"I'll keep Bryony here for the night," said Miss Cameron firmly. "She can sleep in my spare bedroom. And I have a telephone by my bed, so don't hesitate to ring me the moment you have any news."

"I'll do that."

"Do you want to speak to Bryony?"

"Just to say good night."

Miss Cameron shut herself in the kitchen while father and daughter talked together. When she heard the ring of the receiver being replaced, she did not go out into the hall, but busied herself at the sink, filling hot-water bottles and wiping down the already immaculate draining board. She half-expected tears when Bryony joined her, but Bryony was as composed and dry-eyed as ever.

"He says we just have to wait. Do you mind if I stay the night with you? I can go next door and get my toothbrush and things."

"I want you to stay. You can sleep in my spare room."

Bryony finally went to bed, with a hot-water bottle and a tumbler of warm milk. Miss Cameron went to say good night, but she was too shy to stoop and kiss her. Bryony's flame of hair was spread like red silk on Miss Cameron's best linen pillowcase, and she had brought an aged teddy bear along with the toothbrush. The teddy had a threadbare nose and only one eye. Half an hour later, when she herself went to bed, she looked in and saw that Bryony was fast asleep.

Miss Cameron lay between the sheets, but sleep did not come easily. Her brain seemed to be wound up with memories, people and places that she had not thought about in years.

"I think everybody's interesting," Bryony had said and Miss Cameron's heart lifted in hope for the state of the world. Nothing could be too bad if there were still young people who thought that way.

"She said you have a beautiful face." Perhaps, she thought, I don't do enough.

I have allowed myself to become too self-contained. It is selfish not to think more about other people. I must do more. I must try to travel. I shall get in touch with Dorothy after the New Year and see if she would like to come with me.

Madeira. They could go to Madeira. There would be blue skies and bougain-villaea. And jarcaranda trees . . .

She awoke with a terrible start in the middle of the night. It was pitch-dark, it was bitterly cold. The telephone was ringing. She put out a hand and turned on the bedside light. She looked at her clock and saw that it was not the middle of the night, but six o'clock in the morning. Christmas morning. She picked up the telephone.

"Yes?"

"Miss Cameron. Ambrose Ashley here . . ." He sounded exhausted.

"Oh." She felt quite faint. "Tell me."

"A little boy. Born half an hour ago. A lovely little boy."

"And your wife?"

"She's asleep. She's going to be fine."

After a little, "I'll tell Bryony," said Miss Cameron.

"I'll get back to Kilmoran some time this morning—around midday, I should think. I'll ring the hotel and take you both there for lunch. That is, if you'd like to come?"

"How kind," said Miss Cameron. "How very kind."

"You're the kind one," said Mr. Ashley.

A new baby. A new baby on Christmas morning. She wondered if they would call it Noel. She got up and went to the open window. The morning was black and cold, the tide high, the inky waves lapping at the sea-wall. The icy air smelt of the sea. Miss Cameron took a deep breath of it, and felt, all at once, enormously excited and filled with boundless energy. A little boy. She revelled in a great sense of accomplishment, which was ridiculous because in fact she had accomplished nothing.

Dressed, she went downstairs to put a kettle on to boil. She laid a tea-tray for Bryony and put two cups and saucers upon it.

I should have a present, she told herself. It's Christmas and I have nothing to give her. But she knew that with the tea-tray she was taking Bryony the best present she had ever had.

Now, it was nearly seven. She went upstairs and into Bryony's room, set the tray down on the bedside table and turned on the lamp. She went to draw the curtains. In the bed, Bryony stirred. Miss Cameron went to sit by her, to take her hand. The teddy was visible, its ears beneath Bryony's chin. Bryony's eyes opened. She saw Miss Cameron sitting there, and at once they were wide and filled with apprehension.

Miss Cameron smiled. "Happy Christmas."

"Has my father rung?"

"You've got a baby brother, and your mother's safe and sound."

"Oh . . ." It was too much. Relief opened the floodgates, and all Bryony's anxieties were released in a torrent of tears. "Oh . . ." Her mouth went square as a bawling child's, and Miss Cameron could not bear it. She could not remember when she had last had physical, loving contact with another human being, but now she opened her arms and gathered the weeping girl up into them. Bryony's arms came round her neck and Miss Cameron was held so closely and so tightly that she thought she would choke. She felt the thin shoulders beneath her hands; the wet cheek, streaming with tears, was pressed against her own.

"I thought . . . I thought something awful was going to happen. I thought she was going to die."

"I know," said Miss Cameron. "I know."

* * *

$\mathcal{I}$t took a little time for them both to recover. But at last it was over, the tears mopped up, the pillows plumped, the tea poured, and they could talk about the baby.

"I'm certain," said Bryony, "that it is terribly *special* to be born on Christmas Day. When shall I see them?"

"I don't know. Your father will tell you."

"When's he coming?"

"He'll be here in time for lunch. We're all going out to the hotel to eat roast turkey."

"Oh, good. I'm glad you're coming too. What shall we do till he comes? It's only half past seven."

"There's lots to do," said Miss Cameron. "We've got to have a great big breakfast, and light a great big Christmas fire. And if you'd like to, we could go to church."

"Oh, let's. And sing carols. I don't mind thinking about Christmas now. I didn't want to think about it last night." She said, "I suppose I couldn't have a simply boiling-hot bath, could I?"

"You can do anything you like." She stood up and picked up the tea-tray and carried it to the door. But as she opened the door, Bryony said, "Miss Cameron," and she turned back.

"You were so sweet to me last night. Thank you so much. I don't know what I would have done if you hadn't been there."

"I liked having you," said Miss Cameron truthfully. "I liked talking." She hesitated. An idea had just occurred to her. "Bryony, after all we've been through together, I don't really think you should go on calling me Miss Cameron. It sounds so very formal, and after all, we're past that now, aren't we?"

Bryony looked a little surprised, but not in the least put out.

"All right. If you say so. But what *shall* I call you?"

"My name," said Miss Cameron, and found herself smiling, because, really, it was a very pretty name, "is Isobel."

Acknowledgements

We thank all the members of the Pilcher family for their assistance and support. And we should also like to thank all those who have contributed to the success of this book, especially:
Sophie Duncker
Sara Lithgow
Constance and Michael Smith

Picture Credits

All photographs by Andreas von Einsidel, except the following:
iv, ITTC / The Image Bank (TIB); vi, Konrad Wothe / LOOK; 3, old postcard; 4, Lynn M. Stone / The Image Bank / TIB; 5, (1) Patti McConville / TIB, (2) John P. Kelly / TIB, (3) Marc Romanelli / TIB, (4) Peter Miller / TIB; 7, Steve Martin; 9, The Carbis Bay Hotel; 10, Steve Dunwell / TIB; 11, (1) Grant Faint / TIB, (2) Frans Lemmens / TIB; 13, Stuart Hall / Tony Stone; 14, Steve Martin; 16, Murray Alcosser / TIB; 19, Joseph Devenney / TIB; 24, 25, 53, Private property of Rosamunde Pilcher; 50, Laurence Dutton / Tony Stone; 54, Tom Owen Edmunds / TIB; 73, Paul Webster / Tony Stone; 78-79, The Tom Smith Group Ltd., Norwich; 84, Kathy Collins / Robert Harding Picture Library; 87, Joe Devenny / TIB; 88, Lisl Dennis / TIB; 91, Herb Hartmann / TIB; 92, Trevor Wood / Tony Stone; 95, ITTC / TIB; 98, Schulenburg / The Interior Archives; 103, Karl Johaentges / LOOK; 104, Patti McConville / TIB; 107, Renate Kupatt / TIB; 108, Romilly Lockyer / TIB; 110, David Sutherland / Tony Stone; 113, John Netherton / TIB; 117, MS Images / TIB; 120, Robert Harding Picture Library; 122, Christel Rosenfeld / Tony Stone

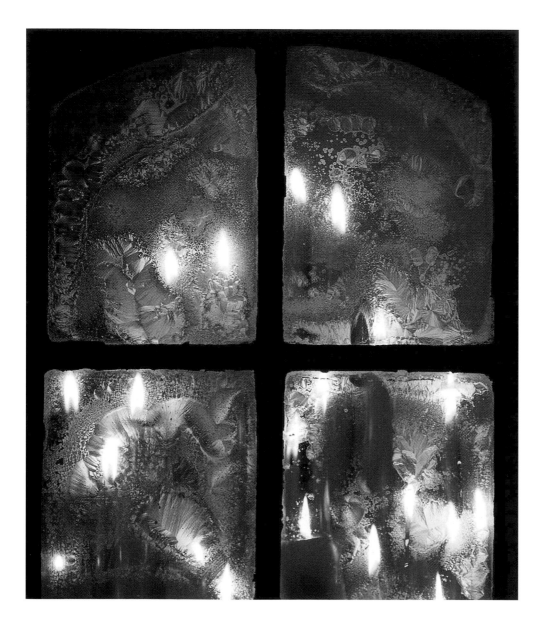